LEADERSHIP

Hernessing human leadership capabilities

TABLE OF CONTENTS

CHAPTER 1

WHAT IS LEADERSHIP?

With a title like that you might think 'I' bit off a little more than 'I' can chew. You might be right, but because there are literally thousands of articles, blogs and websites dedicated to discussions of leadership, I wanted to offer a logical definition of it in a thousand words or less. Here goes...

Despite the multiplicity of interpretations we read every day, leadership can be defined simply as:

"Organizing a group of people to achieve a common goal"

A leader can be anyone. There is no need for any formal authority to lead. A person simply needs to have the will, the courage, the charisma and the ability to capture the imagination of one or more followers in order to be considered a leader.

Centuries ago, it was assumed that good and powerful leaders had naturally occurring leadership traits that set them apart from others...Hence, the term, "leaders are born not made". However, more recent studies have made it clear that given the right set of circumstances and with the appropriate motivation, most people can become true and effective leaders.

Some of the naturally occurring traits that make leadership ability come more easily to some people are:

- Intelligence
- Assertiveness
- Diligence
- Openness
- Courage

When those instinctive traits are combined with learned skills and natural talents, variable levels of leadership ability may be reached. Without all of those traits, effective leadership is possible but much more difficult to achieve.

"It is important to note that one can lead much more effectively when the leadership endeavour involves something that the leader has good expertise in so that he or she may set an example"

It must also be something in which the followers have a need for or an interest in being lead in. For example: An expert tennis player might make a great tennis coach but a lousy sales manager. In addition, there would be no point in trying to lead someone to better customer service skills when he or she works in the depths of a coal mine.

As trite as those examples might seem, it is not unusual that people are put into leadership positions that they are not capable of handling simply because they have done well in another unrelated area. Also, self-promoting or toxic people who have no business trying to lead will often attempt to influence or lead coworkers in inappropriate directions. Both situations will create poor results.

"Good and powerful leaders need to have self-awareness and a solid grip on their own emotions"

Leadership skill necessarily includes the ability to set a mood or tone for the team. Leaders unavoidably telegraph their moods and attitudes to their followers who will adopt the preeminent emotional tone of the leader and carry it throughout the organization.

"One must not assume the only way to achieve financial success or even team success is through servant leadership, participative leadership, or compassionate leadership"

Given the right impetus and favourable circumstances an autocratic, command and control leader can drive his team to success both in the business world, on a sports court or on a battlefield. In the twenty-first century, we tend to reject that style of leadership, but it can be an effective (albeit, potentially negative and harmful) form of leadership nonetheless. If the team is not engaged and motivated, a strong autocrat might be the only leader who can create the environment needed for success.

Modern leadership lecturers and writers also reject the term "management", since it seems to imply a lack of compassion and favours transactional or task orientation as opposed to transformational or people-oriented leadership. In reality, all organizations have some form of tasks and a specific number of people so it is evident that management may still be an integral part of the leadership cycle in many cases.

"In essence, even bad leadership is a form of leadership"

The efficacy of any leadership style can only be measured in results. In other words if the team meets or exceeds all of its goals, under the direction of its leader, those who benefit from those results may assume that the leadership was good regardless of the leader's style. However, it is important to note that bad leadership in any form is usually short-lived.

The best and generally, most effective form of leadership occurs when a leader is able to maintain a high level of concern for his or her people while simultaneously keeping high-level performance paramount in the minds of all participants. This form of leadership often goes a step beyond servant leadership because it allows the leader to accurately control production and monitor results for maximum success. A leader who can juggle tasks and people without sacrificing integrity for either is a great leader indeed. That leader will almost always turn out better performance, more production and measurable growth while presiding over happy, well-engaged employees.

"It is important to recognize that groups of working people are assembled primarily to create some sort of product or service"

Great leaders are able to create buy-in to the vision of the organization while accepting and embracing the direction of its leaders. The key to buy-in and strong followership is communication.

Great Leaders are Great Communicators!

Ten ways to recognize a great leader:

1. Great leaders create a sense of unity amongst all team members.

2. Great leaders have strong interpersonal skills and they encourage interpersonal communication amongst team members.

3. Great leaders have the ability to create a unanimous desire amongst team members to achieve common goals.

4. Great leaders communicate their vision to their team enthusiastically.

5. Great leaders constantly seek feedback from team members.

6. Great leaders never stop learning new leadership techniques.

7. Great leaders set fair and reasonable performance standards and assist team members in achieving them.

8. Great leaders set a conscientious, diligent example for the team.

9. Great leaders never settle for mediocrity from themselves or from their team.

10. Great leaders give credit for great results to the team.

What is leadership?

"Leadership is the embodiment of the positive dynamics evident in all great human relationships within one person or leadership team!"

GENERAL IDEA OF LEADERSHIP

If you have attended any kind of management training, be it management training courses or management training programs you might have noticed that all of them focus on leadership. Management training courses and management training programs may even give out materials like pamphlets or booklets on the subject. And, you take it all promising to read it but of course forget about it completely the moment you are out of the room. What is leadership really about? Does a leader really need to attend management training courses and management training programs? The answer is yes and no. It all depends on the person and the management.

You ask hundred people about leadership and you will get hundred different answers but all the answers will have this point in common. Simply, that a leader is a person who leads. And that is really the truth. But, what is it about? Is it simply about leading people or there are lots of other factors that come into play? This is what management training focuses on. Management training courses and management training programs are all about this.

First of all let's be clear - there are no hard and fast rules that you can follow to become a good leader. If there were rules the management training courses and management training programs would be telling you about these rules and all of us would be leaders by now. But, there are certain skills a person possesses by virtue of which he or she becomes a leader. The funniest part of being a leader is that you may not even know that you are a leader or that you possess the skills to lead. For a leader it is just natural to lead and others follow.

Any management training program will tell you that leadership means responsibility. A leader is a person who is ready to take responsibility - for the group, for the task he or she has to do. This means that others will look up to you to show how things are done, take initiative to solve problems. It also means you will be the first person to be called in case of a crisis. This is not just true for the management of a company but true in other fields as well. A football captain who leads his team to victory, a leader of a country who leads her country to prosperity or a scout leading his team; are all leaders. They are all ready to take responsibility.

The way a leader leads varies from person to person. Remember that after all, a leader is also a human being. And each human being is unique in his/her way. How a person leads depends on basically three things - the leader, the group that is being led and the situation. An effective leader is one, who is alert to the reactions of the group, is aware of the circumstances around him and is aware of is abilities and reactions.

So, does this mean only people with natural skills can become good leaders? Can others acquire these skills? The answer to the first question is no and the second question is yes. Just like, you can learn to swim or any other skill for that matter, you can learn to become a good leader. That is why we have so many management training programs and management training courses. They are meant not just to hone the skills of a natural leader but also to train others to become good leaders. You can of course try and develop these skills on your own but how are you going to know whether your learning is effective or not. For that you need the help of a professional. Only a trained professional can gauge you and train you to grab the niceties of effective leadership. There are many management training programs out there which can help you out. So, next time your company signs you up for a management training program or a management training course, be grateful for the opportunity and grab it with both hands. Keep in mind that these programs can make you a better leader. Don't lose it or waste it away. You may not get another chance.

DIFFERENT TYPES OF LEADERSHIP

Leadership can be characterized in different ways. Sometimes the focus is on leadership styles while at other times the focus is on the characteristics of a leader. Yet, another way to look at types of leadership is by organizational levels. Leading at different levels of an organization requires a leader to use a different approach at each level. Thus, it is important for leaders to understand the different types of leadership and what they need to do to be an effective leader at each level. Although complex organizations may have many levels, listed here are the basic types of leadership based on organizational levels:

Self-leadership: Regardless of whether you are leading a small team or a large organization, all leadership endeavors begin with self-leadership. Self-leadership begins with introspection and development of one's emotional intelligence. Leaders must know themselves first before they can effectively lead others.

Individual leadership: Individual leadership is about performance at a high level as an individual contributor. Leadership is not only a function of a position on an organizational chart, but also individual performance. Anyone at any level of an organization can be a leader, even when they are not in a formal leadership position.. Individual leaders are recognized for their leadership in setting the pace and high standards in their work.

Team leadership: Team leadership is the leadership of a small team. It involves direct interaction between the leader and their followers. Generally, the leader is in frequent contact with their team members, and the leader is responsible for everything the team does or fails to do.

Organizational leadership: Organizational leadership is leadership at the intermediate and highest levels of an organization. This type of leadership is indirect leadership because the leaders generally do not have direct contact with everyone in the organization. They lead indirectly by influencing the larger organization through subordinate leaders. They also exert indirect leadership on the whole organization by managing cultural norms, rewards and recognition programs, and communications.

Macro leadership: Macro leadership is the leadership of complex organizations or even political units of government where there are many stakeholders. As difficult as it is to lead a large corporation, it is immeasurably more difficult to lead a city, state, or country as the elected political leader. The leader must lead by building political coalitions and use position power and influence to rally followers to their vision. Perhaps this is the most difficult type of leadership because it is so dependent on the leader's power of persuasion and charisma, even when they hold a lofty office like mayor, governor, prime minister, or president.

Although there are common elements of leadership at all of these levels, there are also important differences. Leaders must use different leadership skills to lead a team, an organization, or a city. For example, team leaders who are promoted into an organizational leadership role will find that the direct leadership skills which they used as a team leader will not work as well at the organizational level. If they can't quickly make the transition and learn how to lead indirectly, they will likely not succeed. It is important for the leader to recognize these differences and understand how they must exercise their leadership. Understanding the different types of leadership will be the difference between success and failure as a leader.

DIFFERENT THOUGHTS AND OPINIONS ON LEADERSHIP

SCHOOL OF THOUGHT 1

Perhaps the shortest and easiest answer to "what is leadership?" is: there is no leadership. At least there is no such thing as the archetypal leader who, as the dictionary says, "is the action of leading a group of people or an organization". Or it is said to be "a state or position of being the leader". What's odd about the definitions is they are both self-referential. The word leader is used to describe what leadership is. Therefore, it never really tells you what a leader is.

Explaining what leadership is may be as challenging as explaining what a word is without using words. Like leadership, word is self-referential.

Perhaps leadership has never had anything to do with others or followers. Perhaps it has more to do with the future you declare. The question is: what future are you declaring? If you're biggest declaration is you will tie your shoes tomorrow, you may not have what it takes to create entirely new futures.

On the other hand, if you possess boldness and commitment, you may declare you will accomplish something so big that you could never do it on your own. For example, Henry Ford declared most households would own a car. To do that, he enlisted a host of very smart people to support that vision. By 1927, most households owned cars in the US. Ford had 60% market share.

On the surface, you may believe that Henry Ford was bossy and told people what to do. That is not leadership. That may have more to do with a person attempting to prove something to themselves or others. In fact, it may be a way to hide inadequacies. However, that is another subject.

Leader's who declare the future also declare who they are. One of the first things they declare is RESPONSIBILITY. If things go wrong, they will deal with the adversity. If people have a hard time seeing the leaders vision, he or she will take the time to create understanding and alignment. Not only are they responsible for the project, they are responsible for how they engage people. They know their vision can, at first, appear impossible.

With that said, one way to distinguish a great leader in your organization is to look for high responsibility and great communication. While there are many people who have great ideas and can be responsible, it is a completely different paradigm when someone is responsible for ensuring understanding and alignment. That takes a high commitment, patience and responsibility to others. In no way am I talking about being a servant leader. I am saying the person who is the leader will be most powerful in the face of adversity or when things are not going as expected. They are more likely to bring order out of chaos, even if that means increasing chaos to achieve order. And they will gladly take responsibility for everything.

When you look at leadership from the perspective of declaring a future, you see a person declaring a future that has not existed. In most cases, the path to a future that does not exist is filled with unforeseen challenges, problems and breakdowns. Those are the very things most avoid. As a result, most declare what they know they can do. A leader, on the other hand, will declare responsibility without anyone asking them to. In addition, the person leading is not necessarily telling others what to do. They are more likely looking at the big picture and asking questions that no one is asking. They are responsible for effective communication for themselves and others. Furthermore, in many cases, they don't have the answers. They may simply have a responsible method for asking questions and getting answers out of others. When this happens, the people may say they did it themselves.

SCHOOL OF THOUGHT 2

Some people will tell you, if you ask them, that they think leadership is deciding on a plan of action and sticking to it, no matter what. Others will tell you it means taking charge of a situation and then handing out tasks so everything gets done right and by the set deadline. What if that's not leadership? What if leadership is less about handing out orders and sticking by a plan whether or not it works and more about working with people to mentor them and help them find their own path. I would argue that defining a leader today is much different than it was 5 or 10 years ago. In fact, I would say that inspiration is the biggest thing you contribute to a company or even a person when you become a leader.

While leaders are made, most are born. That sounds odd, doesn't it? Well, the truth is we can't all be leaders and not everyone wants to be a leader. There are many responsibilities attached to leadership. No matter what anyone else is doing, when you're the leader, you are in charge and the results you deliver, whether they're good or bad, are a direct reflection of your work and efforts. Honestly, most people are genuinely scared of failure. Leaders are not.

Natural born leaders know that you miss opportunities and blessings when you avoid failure. Not that failure is something to strive for because it's not. However, people who are trying to avoid failure, typically avoid doing things or taking risks in the first place. Did you know that Thomas Edison tried 5,000 times to invent a working light bulb before he actually created one that worked? Do you realize that what that actually means is he failed 5,000 times? That's a lot of failure and yet he's known, as it should be, for his inventions, his light bulb.

Think of some well-known leaders or business owners. Let's look at Donald Trump. He's a business owner, a billionaire and a leader. He has also failure. Repeatedly. More than once his failure has cost him everything or nearly everything. So what makes Trump special and why does he stand out? He's a leader who believes in, and inspires the best in his people. He pushes people to excel, to get better at whatever they're good at. He pushes them to risk failure because he knows that that's where the greatest successes come from.

At the end of the day, people who inspire, people who take risks, people who are willing to try, and fail; those are the ones you want to follow because they believe in themselves, they take risks, they believe in their goal and they believe in other people and their potential. True leaders, the people who will get in the trenches with you, those are the people you should follow if you want to succeed. You are one of those people.

SCHOOL OF THOUGHTS 3

Leadership is an interactive conversation that pulls people toward becoming comfortable with the language of personal responsibility and commitment.

Leadership is not just for people at the top. Everyone can learn to lead by discovering the power that lies within each one of us to make a difference and being prepared when the call to lead comes.

Albert Einstein once said, "We should take care not to make the intellect our god; it has, of course, powerful muscles but no personality. It cannot lead; it can only serve." Leaders know and science has discovered emotionality's deeper purpose: the timeworn mechanisms of emotion allow two human beings to receive the contents of each person's minds. Emotion is the messenger of love; it is the vehicle that carries every signal from one brimming heart to another.

Leadership is applicable to all facets of life: a competency that you can learn to expand your perspective, set the context of a goal, understand the dynamics of human behavior and take the initiative to get to where you want to be.

Here are five guiding principles that guide respectful conversations:

1. When peers connect change happens. Effective coaching can happen on the dance floor of conversation.

2. It's OK to begin a conversation by confronting the other person with questions that seem awkward but set the stage for a respectful exchange. Why waste time on small talk? Just ask to-the-point information-seeking questions, like: "What are you here for? How do you want to spend our time together?"

3. Conversations are not meant to be structured. Be open to conversations that you are unprepared for and focused on the interests of the other person (not your purpose).

4. Don't get pulled into solving problems that may not matter to the other person. Allow time for the person to get to what's really important. Provide spaces where they can express their doubts and fears by being a thoughtful listener--without taking on the responsibility to fix or debate the issue. After all, you have invited the person to talk about what matters to her or him, not you, so allow time for the articulation of those thoughts and feelings.

5. Personal transformation happens when the right questions get asked--not by providing answers. When you focus on the solution, you are trying to sell the person something. When you allow people to answer their own questions, they discover what they were not aware of---and what is needed to move forward. Personal transformation leads corporate transformation--one person at a time.

That is why leadership development is not an event. It is a process of participating in respectful conversations where the leader recognizes his or her own feelings and those of others in building safe and trusting relationships. For human beings, feeling deeply is synonymous with being alive.

LEADERSHIP AS AN OPPORTUNITY, RATHER THAN A POSITION

"Leadership is an opportunity to serve. It is not a trumpet call to self-importance"

– J. Donald Walters

Many equate leadership only with formal position. This approach tends to assume the accumulation of time in place is equivalent to leadership development and that promotion should be made primarily on seniority. Despite this prevailing view, true leadership is a way of thinking regardless of position or formal authority. Leadership is about doing the consistent, hidden work of self-improvement in the areas of high-trust relationships, paradigms examination, long-term analysis and continuous improvement through creativity and innovation. Leadership is more about "them" and the organization at large rather than just "me."

The opportunity to serve a large crowd or even a small group of people is given to only few and as such, leading them should be acknowledged as a privilege, rather than seen as a position. It's your turn to lead today and would most likely be someone else's turn tomorrow. What you do and how you serve them during your tenure will go down in history as what you have offered to the people you served. When you are given the chance to serve, it's important that you draw value to yourself, however, this shouldn't be about pride and ego which would mostly likely feel way above others or see yourself as better than them. Always remember that power is like a grain of sand held in hand; the more you force your hands on it, the more you lose. The question is why chose to lose your value in such way rather than being praised for your steadfastness, accountability, leading by example and most important, your interpersonal relationship with others?

WHO IS A LEADER?

A leader is a person who leads others, giving them direction and showing the way for others to follow. A leader must have a commanding influence. A leader makes people do what they don't like to do and make them enjoy doing it. The leader leaves nothing to chance, he daily fine-tunes his leadership skills. Having carefully thought out his plan of action, the leader deliberately exerts special influence. His vision is deliberate (Even when he receives a divine call he responds). His choice of group is deliberate. His selection of goals is deliberate his assessment of the real needs of the group is deliberate. Leadership is the discipline of deliberately exerting special influence within a group to move it toward goals of beneficial permanence that fulfill the groups real needs. Leadership is a discipline. It is hard work. It takes effort and concentration, it takes staying power. Leadership is deliberate.

As a leader of an organization, you need to be very careful the type of people you attract. If the folks you are attracting are not the ilk you would like, often there is either something wrong with your message or there is a real problem with your personal character. If a leader is attracting too many criminals, questionable characters, malcontents, or folks with terrorist like tendencies, then that leader needs greater scrutiny.

Of course, leaders are often put under a microscope and when they are, it's just amazing what you will find. In fact, a leader needs to be careful that they do not associate and attract followers or crazies, as their biggest fans. Why you ask? Well, people often judge you by the company you keep and you know what they say; "You are a collage of your five closest friends."

More than one great leader, politician, or corporate executive has been ruined due to their associates and "go to guys," in fact, in the 2008 Presidential Election we saw this play out and it was all over the media for months on end and almost changed the outcome of the election. This is a prime example of one of the traps that leaders can fall into.

So, every great leader must ask themselves; "who am I attracting and why?" Then they must take appropriate action to shield themselves from such questionable followers and modify their tone. Otherwise the leader might be labeled as a malcontent themselves, have their reputations tarnished, and lose trust with those they lead. So, please consider this.

DIFFERENT THOUGHTS ON WHO IS A LEADER

SCHOOL OF THOUGHT 1

Many individuals consider themselves leadership material. When asked, they will often offer all the rhetoric and platitudes that far too many associate with being a leader. They use all the catchy phrases and jargon that they learn from books, seminars, or some self- appointed leadership gurus. Perhaps one of the best summations of what being a leader is really all about was said by John C. Maxwell, when he said, "A leader is one who knows the way, goes the way, and shows the way."

1. What does Maxwell mean by "knows the way?" Leadership expertise arrives from many years of training, learning, and development. Training alone does not make someone a leader, unless they are also willing to convert that training into actual learning, by understanding it, questioning, and getting valuable experience. This, in turn, creates an atmosphere of gaining knowledge from those experiences, and productive knowledge and meaningful experiences combined with developed skills are the basic ingredients in creating the wisdom required to develop valuable expertise.

2. All that knowledge alone still does not make someone a leader. That is where Maxwell's "goes the way" comes in. In evaluating if someone will potentially become a true and effective leader, observe whether they merely talk about things, or if they instead lead the way by showing others what needs to be done, and leading by example. Only when others realize that a leader feels strongly enough about something to get his hands dirty and be hands on, will they feel comfortable in following? The adage that actions speak louder than words is even more relevant when it comes to real leadership.

3. Unless a leader is willing to communicate openly and motivate others to action, he is not fulfilling his duty as a leader. Showing the way involves opening the eyes of others to accept your vision as important enough to adopt as their own.

There are many phases involved in becoming a great leader. There are no shortcuts, or half- way methods of doing this properly. It takes commitment, vision, belief, inner strength, absolute integrity, and an overwhelming desire to create value for others.

SCHOOL OF THOUGHT 2

Have you ever observed any particular individual, serving in a position of leadership, and wondered, where their allegiance was, and whether, their priority, was serving their organization and constituents, or, merely, their personal agenda, and/ or self - interest? In the process of considering who a leader actually represents and serve, let's attempt to briefly consider, examine, review, and discuss, using the mnemonic approach, why this is, such an essential aspect, of quality, relevant, inspiring, motivating, meaningful, effective leadership.

1. Strengthen; solutions; sustainable system: One must do, everything possible, to consistently strengthen, the group he serves, and constituents he represents, or, he isn't a real leader! This means avoiding the easier path, often traveled, of using empty rhetoric, and promising (without fulfilling), and seeking well - considered, viable solutions. The strategic and action plans must be, both, relevant, to address current challenges, and obstacles, while focusing on the future, by perceiving and conceiving of, creating, developing, and implementing, the finest possible, sustainable system!

2. Empathy; energy: A real leader must, seek to inspire and motivate his stakeholders, in order to attract them, to become more involved and committed. When the process begins with effectively listening, and consistently, learning from every conversation and experience, he becomes capable of proceeding with genuine empathy! Combing this, with the energy, to persist, when lesser individuals, do not, often differentiates quality leaders, from the rest of the pack!

3. Relevant; reliable; reasoning: How much time and effort, one, uses, and puts in, to meaningful, relevant, reasoning,

often determines the level of one's performance, and their ability to be a reliable leader!

4. Vision; views; value; values: If you want to lead, it's important to introspectively, objectively, consider your reasons, and whether, your vision, is one, which will serve the best interests of the group! Will your views be, both, of relevant value, as well as maintain a commitment to the heritage and values of your organization and stakeholders?

5. Emphasis; excellence: How someone determines, and places his emphasis, often differentiates, and distinguishes, between pseudo - leaders, and the few individuals, who will be relevant leaders! One must maintain his commitment to performing with the utmost personal excellence, while always thanking others, for their service, and participation!

Wouldn't every group, be better served, if their leaders focused on them, and did everything, possible, to consistently SERVE their organization, and stakeholders, best interests? Will you be up to the task?

DIFFERENT TYPES OF LEADERS

"Leadership" seems to be one of those words that is thrown around today in a much over-used fashion. Not unlike "success" and "motivational" and "outside the box." What the heck do those words really mean? The answer lies in a slight variation of that question; what do those words mean TO YOU?

Type 1: Managerial Leader

A managerial leader is the least effective of the five types of leaders. They have the least influence. People only follow them because they have to. They are not in the position to serve others. Their desire is to be served by others because they are in the position. They see others as tools to use to complete the objective for the day. They prefer to make decisions. Their weakness is character development.

Here's a brief review of characteristics:

• Character is weak.

• Desire is "to be served" rather than "to serve."

• They have a scarcity mindset.

• Competency can range from undeveloped to highly¬-developed.

• Focus is on managing (directing/controlling) people and processes.

• Values the position more than the people.

• Strength comes from power, control, formal authority, and personal results.

Type 2: Relational Leader

A relational leader builds relationships in order to influence others. People want to follow them because of who they are, not what they know. They develop mutual respect with others and work well with them. Although people want to follow them, they have not developed specialized knowledge. Their weakness is not making the necessary sacrifices to develop their competency.

Here's a brief review of characteristics:

• Character is strong.

• Desire is to serve.

• They have an abundance mindset.

• Competency is undeveloped and generalized.

• Focus is on leading (influencing/releasing) people.

• Values people more than the position.

• Strength comes from relationships and moral authority.

Type 3: Motivational Leader

A motivational leader seeks mutual benefit for themselves, others, and the organization. People want to follow them because of who they are and what they know. They influence others from the outside. They are process focused. They are trusted and deliver results for themselves, their families, their team, their organization, their customers, their suppliers, and their community. Their weakness is not making the necessary sacrifices to reproduce other motivational leaders.

Here's a brief review of characteristics:

• Character is strong.

• Desire is to serve.

• They have an abundance mindset.

• Competency is developed and specialized.

• Focus is on leading (influencing/releasing) people, managing the processes, and getting results.

• Values people more than the position.

• Strength comes from relationships, moral authority, and team results.

Type 4: Inspirational Leader

An inspirational leader inspires managerial and relational leaders to become motivational leaders. Their focus is on growing themselves in order to inspire others to grow. They influence others on the inside. They are people-focused not process-focused. They focus heavily on character development. True inspirational leaders are followed because of how much they care and who they are on the inside. They are inspired by the growth of those following them.

Here's a brief review of characteristics:

• Character is stronger.

• Desire is to serve and develop others.

• They have an abundance mindset.

• Competency is highly developed and specialized.

• Focus is on leading (influencing/releasing) people and developing motivational leaders.

• Values people more than the position.

• Strength comes from relationships, moral authority, and the growth of others.

Type 5: Transformational Leader

A transformational leader's passion and purpose is to transform others. They are the most influential of the five types of leaders and are highly respected. Their reputation precedes them. They are well known for developing leaders. Their influence touches people in all industries and across multiple generations. They have influenced many leaders for many years. Their influence is continuously being transferred through many other leaders at many different times in multiple locations.

Here's a brief review of characteristics:

• Character is strongest.

• Desire is to serve and to develop others.

• They have an abundance mindset.

• Competency is highly developed and specialized.

• Focus is on leading (influencing/releasing) people and developing motivational and inspirational leaders.

• Values people more than the position.

• Strength comes from relationships, moral authority, growth of others, and the respect they have earned.

WHAT IT MEANS TO SERVE BY EXAMPLE

Leadership is not something that can be turned on and off for convenience or for taking the easy way out of responding to a particular situation. Leading by example simply means creating a path which your followers can follow. As a leader, there's always a group of people that looks up to you and serving them is what is expected of you. Serving them or leading isn't the real deal, but leading them by example. Can your followers take after you? Can they follow your path? What examples are you laying down for them? These are the basic and simple questions you should ask yourself.

As a leader, it isn't until when you gather a group of people or have certain number of people who follows you or look up to you that you becomes one, it starts from the simplest level; in the family. As a father, you are leader to your children, as the eldest child, you are a leader to your other siblings. That's how the chain goes till it gets to the highest level.

Leadership requires a commitment to continually educate and develop yourself, nurturing complex relationships and earning the respect of those you lead, those you follow, and those who either regularly or occasionally are part of your life. The journey begins inside. Therefore, the first person you must lead before you can lead others is yourself. Leaders are defined by their choices, decisions and attitudes. In these tumultuous times, what comes to the surface so often is the global crisis-level deficit of positive, ethical, and effective leadership. A reversal of this crisis can only be reversed one individual at a time. Be the change you wish to see in the world.

Developing the foresight and discipline to lead yourself, and lead others by your example, is the hallmark of a true leader. You must strive to be part of the solution, not part of the problem, and work with a positive let's-make-it-happen attitude. With every moment of every day, as you build your own road to success, ask yourself: Is this action building a wall that holds others back or a bridge that facilitates their advancement?

To serve and lead others by example, lots of responsibilities falls to you and you are expected to possess certain qualities. Some leaders are born-leaders while some only possess certain qualities that makes people call them leaders. Within yourself as a leader, different voice speaks to you especially when it comes to making decisions in hard time.

IMPACTING PEOPLE'S LIFE POSITIVELY AS A LEADER

It's amazing to me how many 'leaders' there are in the world today who have no real, positive influence into people lives. They are in positions of leadership but allow the position to intoxicate them in such a way that they forget that they have the ability to actually impact people and to help them become everything that they can be.

How many times have you known a leader, whether they are a boss, politician, figure- head, or sports icon that, when you meet them, are rude, arrogant, and give you the impression that the world revolves around them? You have to understand that being a leader doesn't mean that you are in a position where you are to be served by humanity for the rest of your life. Actually, you are in a position where you should be serving humanity by paving the way for other people, enabling them to reach their own full potential.

By contrast, have you have met a leader that, when you are around them, they go out of their way to make you feel like you are the most important person in the room? This is a true leader with influence, the influence to impart to people the feelings of worth, respect, and belief in oneself.

According to Samuel Adams, "It does not require a majority to prevail, but rather an irate, tireless minority keen to set brush fires in people's minds." In other words, you don't have to be a leader who shows off their influence with a bunch of pomp and circumstance, rather show your influence to each individual you come across by lighting a brush fire in their mind about how much potential that they have on the inside of them. Make more of an effort to be keen to the lives of other people than you are about yours.

Of course, this approach to leadership is time consuming and requires a bit more effort, but why did you become a leader in the first place? Was it so that you could hoard all the privileges to yourself, or was it so that you could be in a position to impact the people who are in your world? Make a decision today that, from now on, you will use your leadership position to set brush fires of hope, encouragement, and inspiration in everyone you meet, even if it may seem insignificant to you.

THE CHARACTERISTICS OF GOOD LEADERSHIP

Oftentimes, we find it hard to identify the characteristics of good leadership. In one book, a leader is described as the take-charge person who leads his team. In another, you're considered a leader if you empower your subordinates and rely on their own ability to make decisions for the team. There are certain qualities and characteristics expected of individual leaders in other to lead your team to success. It is essential to possess all these characteristics or most of these to serve as an effective good leader.

1. Vision

Good leaders have vision. Good leaders know where they are heading and they lead these people toward the same vision that they have for their lives, a community, or even a nation. They do not just look at what things are, but at what things could be.

2. Passionate

Good leaders are not passive people. They are usually extremely passionate in whatever they're doing. Whether it is sports or business, leaders are extremely focused and some of them are even consumed by their passion.

3. Wise

Good leaders are wise and discerning. Being a leader often means that they need to make crucial decisions at various points in their ministry. Having the wisdom to make the right decision is extremely important in ensuring the success of the organization.

4. Compassion

They have compassion for their followers. While they understand they have a goal to pursue, they constantly look back and care for the people that are following them. They are not selfish people who only think about their own needs and luxuries; they also have a heart for the people under them as well.

5. Charismatic

Good leaders are charismatic; they are attractive people and they draw people to them by their shining personalities. Whether is it the way they speak, or the excellence they demand from people; these leaders have an X-factor that people feel drawn toward.

6. Good Communicators

They are very good at orating and speaking. They are extremely well-versed in public speaking and they can influence and inspire people with the things that they say. With this ability, it is not surprise that they can usually garner a good following.

7. Persistent

They are persistent in reaching their goals. They understand that reaching a destination is filled with setbacks. Despite that, they see that the benefits of reaching the goal is greater than that of the setback that they experienced. This makes them extremely persistent people.

8. Integrity

Good leaders have integrity. They mean what they say, and they say what they mean. They are people who keep their promises and they don't play the two-faced political game that a lot of others do. As such, people find them trustworthy and they give their commitment to these leaders as a result.

9. Courageous

They are courageous. Winston Churchill says that courage is the virtue on which all others virtue rest upon. Besides just having a pipe dream, good leaders are courageous enough to pursue after it. The fears are real, but a courageous leader pursues them despite the fears.

10. Disciplined

Good leaders are extremely disciplined in their pursuit of their goals. While most people would be easily distracted or discouraged, good leaders discipline their flesh to keep focused and to keep steady despite the circumstances.

There you go, ten characteristics of good leadership. After reading these ten characteristics, you might see that you are lacking in some areas and strong in others. But no matter, it's not about becoming perfect, but knowing where you are lacking and making an effort to develop those characteristics in yourself.

SETTING LEADERSHIP GOALS

Leaders know where they are going; they have plans in place to get them there; they know what will be required to achieve their goals and most importantly they approach there journey with a level of vigor and enthusiasm that is contagious and excites all who are involved.

As a leader are you satisfied with where you have been heading; energized about what you are doing or do you find yourself achieving goals set for you by others?

Effective leadership requires clear, concise and continuous movement towards goals that will foster the level of personal and organizational excellence that is associated with leadership brilliance. Goal setting is clearly, the most basic competent of identifying the where, how and why of leadership excellence.

Goal Setting Made Simple, a basic recipe for success

1. First and foremost it is essential that goals you intend to pursue are your goals; it is critical that you understand what you want and who you want to become. Our goals should not be driven by the expectation of others.

2. In establishing our goals it is essential that we state our goals positively and specifically; to be motivated by our goals we must be able to clearly develop a mental picture of doing and achieving what we want to do.

3. Next your goals must be realistic, attainable and measurable; these are goals, which you are willing to work towards, because you believe them to be realistic and achievable. If it cannot be measured then does it really exist? Vague statements of purpose are like trying to hit a moving target, with your eyes closed, difficult if not impossible.

Understand that true success comes from within; many are fearful of the future because they are unsure of what it will bring; they become pawns in the game of life; there movement depends on decisions of others; they relinquish their freedom of choice by having to depend on others to know what to think or do. Remember that people who have goals and plans dictate to others, while people who have no goals or plans are dictated to.

As a leader, the ultimate measure of your success or otherwise is the results that you deliver.

Whether it is fair or not, the reality is that if you don't deliver results, you are unlikely to continue in your role, especially at the most senior levels.

So why should you bother with goal setting?

Provides Focus

When you sit down and clearly define the results or outcomes you are going to deliver, it gives you a very clear focus. With clarity of focus, you are more conscious about where you invest your time and energies, what you do and what you delegate, what types of people you need to support you to deliver results, to name just a few.

Provides Motivation

I don't know about you but for me and for most people who are leaders, there is something really motivating about achieving goals or making progress towards a goal.

Breaking the overall goal into smaller steps provides positive motivation and keeps you moving forward.

Start To Get Results

When you start to focus and stay motivated, you start to deliver results. For most of us, delivering a result acts as a catalyst for us questioning whether we could achieve the next result. Career is a good example: as you start to master a job at a certain level, you start to think about whether you could get results at the next level.

Confidence

Every time that you achieve a result, you are building your confidence and self-belief. We all, no matter who we are, have our periods of self-doubt. Confident people break through this, knowing that setbacks are just part of the journey to success.

Growth

When you set new and challenging goals, you more than likely move outside of your current circle of knowledge or comfort. Every time you do this, you learn something which might be a skill but could just as easily be something about yourself. Once we stop growing, we start stagnating and, when we start stagnating, our productivity and results diminish.

The Bottom Line

Goal setting of the wish list variety won't make much difference. Goal setting with intention, desire and drive on the other hand can hugely influence the success you have as a leader.

CHAPTER 2

LEAD BY CREATING A CULTURE OF CHARACTER

Culture is simply "how we do things here," a set of beliefs and habits that influence how people behave. Culture forms over time and determines what happens when authorities are not present, setting the tone for the organization and the norms for acceptable behavior. Every organization has a culture, explicit or implicit. Explicit is better because it means the leaders understand the importance of culture and are paying attention to it.

A healthy culture doesn't guarantee success, but it provides the foundation for building an excellent, ethical, and enduring organization. It's called culture of character.

The inspiring people who lead with integrity, move things forward, garner commitment from others and are willing to ask the tough questions when necessary are the real leaders who generate and sustain cultures of character in organizations.

What is the essence of your character, who are you really? We all lead from where we stand. Those we lead or those who choose to follow us all see us one way. But are they really seeing the real you? Some have worked with professionals of all levels in which we all have good and outstanding experiences with them, they made us laugh, treated us well enough that we couldn't even ask for more. These are wonderful traits of their character.

So what is leadership character, and how do we build it? The dictionary definition of character is "the mental and moral qualities distinctive to an individual." Notice that the definition didn't talk about technical skills. It instead focuses on the ethical qualities that can provide guidance and a sense of direction when things don't look so promising. Whether heading a team, a department, a company, or, on a larger scale, a country, leaders share some key attributes. The principal traits of leadership, integrity, shared vision, emotional intelligence, positive outlook, authenticity, confidence, forward focus, and listening ability, all converge at the core as character.

The question is what are you character traits? And, probably more importantly, are you showing them to others. Many leaders are seeking the how to tools to engage those around them, taking leadership classes, studying persuasion or using team building exercises. We all know that engagement has a direct effect on how well we feel about our work and greatly impacts performance, profits and sustainability of companies. But what about your character, could that not play a role too? Is it possible that just being human could just be the magic tool you are seeking?

So take a personal scan of your characteristics. Bring them to work with you, then people will discover the uniqueness in you and how pleasurable to have you around. They will turn to you in hard times for advices and involve you in their daily activities, all because they know you are interesting and with good personal qualities, you will become their leader unconsciously and their best friend.

Ever wonder what makes a good leader great? The answer is character.

Character is what flows out of the heart. It is what defines us as a leader. People want to follow people they can look up to and trust. So to become an effective servant leader, we must get intentional about building character. Personal character is the sum of all the qualities that define us as individuals and as leaders. The personal character of leaders defines their depth and stability; it is what leaders are truly made of.

RECOGNIZING CHARACTER

When you look at leaders, you see many things. You can tell easily if they are intelligent, whether they have good technical skills and how much they understand the business and the industry. What you don't see, because it is below the surface in their heart, is their character. Servant leaders are defined and recognizable by their character. Servant leaders know that people will follow them only if they are trusted and trust is only developed through virtuous character.

Servant leadership character traits

Key aspects of a servant leader's heart that will separate them from the pack include:

• The desire to serve others, above and beyond oneself

• Desire for never-ending development of one's ability

• Desire to achieve one's very best

• Willingness to always accept responsibility for one's actions

• Commitment to being humble and vulnerable

• The desire to make a positive impact on society

On-going development

This is not a matter that is looked at only once. It is something we must check up on from time to time. This can be done by asking others (truth tellers) what they think. But don't just stop with the feedback – work to implement changes so you can grow and have a greater impact as a servant leader.

THE CONTROL OF ONE'S EMOTIONS AND IMPULSES

Emotion allows you to be a passionate leader, as long as you are able to balance the emotion or passion with a response that is intellectually appropriate to the situation. The heart and mind, working together, serve as the foundation for leadership that incorporates character and competence: the fusion of emotionally empathetic intellect with knowledge-based skills. Your heart forges the qualities that come more naturally to you, the expressive impact you have on those you lead. Your mind forges your skill, the principles and values you master over time. The two merge to sharpen your response to each challenge.

At one point, or another, most of us, face certain situations, where we are challenged, to remain calm, and clear - headed, because either something, or someone, does, and/ or says something, which makes us want to behave impulsively, and react, often, without fully considering the alternatives, and/ or ramifications. A true leader, however, realizes, he must never, merely, react, until/ unless he, first, fully consider his options, so he can proceed, in the best possible manner. With this in mind, this article will briefly examine, and discuss, using the mnemonic approach, why this is important, and how, quality leaders strive, consistently, to control their IMPULSES.

1. Intelligence; ideas; integrity; imagination; intents: The measure of one's intelligence, should be, whether he is capable of examining, what has been, is (presently), and what should be, and to proceed, with a quality, relevant imagination, focused on perceiving and conceiving of, creating, and developing, relevant, sustainable ideas, rather than merely reacting to circumstances (impulsively)! When one proceeds with a genuine commitment, to maintaining

absolute integrity, and his intentions are pure and focused, on balancing his logical and emotional components, he handles, whatever might challenge him, and/ or present a potential obstacle!

2. Motivate; mention; make mark: If you hope to be a true leader, how will you ensure, you make your mark, for the better? Will your goal, be to motivate and inspire others, to join you, in your quest? Are you willing to, and capable, of mentioning others, and thanking them for their participation, etc?

3. Planning; priorities; perception: One of the significant reasons, organizations benefit, from committing, to developing and implementing, a relevant, leadership planning program, is it creates more capable leaders, who proceed, with the perception, to plan, according to the priorities of their group, and constituents.

4. Useful; unique: Because overcoming obstacles, is often challenging, groups need leaders, with the unique ability, to provide useful leadership, focused on the best approach, without letting their personal fears, etc, interfere!

5. Listen; learn; leadership: Will you be ready, willing and able, to listen, before speaking and/ or reacting, and

learning from every conversation, and experience, in order to provide, well - considered, sustainable leadership?

6. Strengths; synergy: When one focuses clearly, he becomes capable, of considering, the finest, possible, synergy, of logical and emotional components! When this is done, he attempts to use his and the group's strengths, wisely, while addressing, in a timely manner, any potential weaknesses, and/ or obstacles.

7. Empathy; endurance: When one prioritizes empathy, and realizes, leading is a long - term commitment, he possess the necessary endurance, to overcome, anything, put in his way!

8. Solutions; sustainable system: Shouldn't one attempt to seek viable solutions, which, might, best, position him, to perceive and conceive of, create, develop and implement the most relevant, sustainable system?

Since emotions, might either be beneficial, or detrimental, a wise leader, realizes he must seek to consistently control his IMPULSES, in a positive, relevant, sustainable manner. Will you be up to this task?

HOW TO DEVELOP BETTER EMOTIONAL INTELLIGENCE

Make no mistake! Leadership styles directly impact employee engagement, culture and business productivity. How long an employee stays and how productive they are is dependent on the relationship they have with their leader.

There is an ongoing challenge for leaders to continually improve productivity and staff retention. This can be achieved by improving engagement of their workforce through Emotional Intelligence. If you emotionally engage workers, they are by far more productive.

Emotional Intelligence is about one's ability to perceive, understand, reason with and manage one's own feelings, emotions, mood states and behavior's as well as those of others. It's your ability that helps people cope with frustrations, control emotions and get along with others.

Our moods, feelings, and emotions influence us every day at work - to good or bad effect. Not only do they impact every workplace relationship and interaction, they influence fundamental areas like job satisfaction, engagement, and team morale. Numerous studies have found people high in Emotional Intelligence are happier, healthier and more successful in their business, work and personal relationships.

Being a leader in an organization, it is very important to understand about EMOTIONAL INTELLIGENCE as you are dealing with people in order to achieve your organizational goals. It is about the ability to understand and monitor your own emotions and those of people around you. It enables you to modify your feelings and influence what happens in the place around you. This article will talk about EI and how you can use it effective.

What is EI?

Emotional Intelligence is about self-awareness, self-regulation, self-motivation, empathy and social skill.

- Self-awareness - the ability to be aware of what you are feeling, your strengths and weaknesses.

- Self-regulation - ability to manage one's own emotions and impulses.

- Self-motivation - ability to persist in the face of setback and failures.

- Empathy - ability to sense emotions, feelings, needs of others.

- Social skill - ability to handle the emotions of others.

Why is it important?

By using your emotional intelligence, you can create your own success and learn to control WHAT you feel or HOW you feel. EI will help you to choose the right feeling appropriate to a given situation and skill to communicate these feeling effectively. Aristotle once said that anyone can become angry and it is easy. However, he continued that to be angry with the right person to the right degree at the right time for the right purpose and in the right way is not easy.

How can you utilize?

You can use you Emotional intelligence at workplace by maintaining improved personal health and quality relationship, enhancing personal productivity. It will help you to effectively motivate every employee, to convey you massage to the followers, to resolve conflicts and to reduce stress at workplace.

Practicing some simple activities, you can improve your EI. You can make it easier to connect with your feelings by practicing these simple activities. You should spend more time listening to others, take some regular physical exercises, increase positive feedback to yourself and those around you, work with a mentor or life coach, turn mistakes into energy, start spiritual pursuits, recognize your feelings, be motivated to focus on an emotional goal, avoid people who invalidate you or don't respect your feeling and look for the humor or life lesson in a negative situation.

In summary, you will make a lot of differences by learning how to improve your emotional intelligence. What is most important is that you must practice, discipline and keep your honesty always. Then you will grow as an effective leader wherever you may go.

Start developing your Emotional Intelligence TODAY!

HOW TO INSPIRE PEOPLE AND HOW TO ACHIEVE YOUR GOALS

The work place is not made of bricks and machines alone; it is filled with complicated and sensitive human forces.

Extraordinary leaders inspire, energize and muster their followers with extraordinarily few resources because they are genuinely passionate about the well-being of the people under their responsibility. Leadership is defined as the process by which an individual influences a group of individuals to achieve a common goal. Leaders have two main responsibilities: to ensure that the demands of the organisation are satisfied and to ensure that the needs of the people are satisfied.

Leadership is not a combination of traits to be learnt but diverse extreme traits that need to be internalized and leveraged according to situation and context.

The present generation in the business world expects everyone at all levels to demonstrate leadership. As we move forward into networking environment, leaders are expected to be flexible, adaptive and work effectively in teams to handle the new paradigms under conditions of change, uncertainty and complexity.

Demonstrating the qualities of leadership also comes from being committed and passionate towards; not only work but also the people in our work place. Supervisors and managers are required to lead by example and build a common sense of purpose and pride in their teams. They need to be trustworthy and inspire confidence in others so that their team will be motivated to be lead by them.

Being appointed to a position of authority and responsibility does not automatically grant leadership upon the person. To demonstrate leadership, the leader must take the initiative to influence and motivate one another to carry out their tasks confidently and to the best of their ability. Leaders are required to spend time with their teams to get to know them and to fully engage them by explaining their roles, keeping them informed of updates and ensuring that their views are taken into account. Leaders need to also equip themselves with EQ (Emotional Intelligence). In today's work place, it leaders have to recognize, manage and utilize emotions in positive and constructive ways. Emotional Intelligence is also about recognizing other people's emotional states and learning how to engage with them to create an environment of safety, trust and confidence.

A leader needs to be a Coach, Friend, Counselor, Disciplinarian, just to name a few. The fuel that keeps the leadership fire burning is 'Passion' the genuine passion to develop people.

"Leadership is lifting a person's vision to high sights, the raising of a person's performance to a higher standard, the building of a personality beyond its normal limitations." - Peter Drucker.

It is impossible to ever be a truly great leader unless someone is willing and capable of motivating and inspiring others to follow. People only actually follow leaders who provide them with a reason to believe, and motivates them to get more involved, more convinced, and more committed to an organization and/ or some specific cause or need. Having professionally trained and worked with well over a thousand leaders and potential leaders over the last more than three decades, I have come to realize that while it is possible to professionally train someone with the needed skills, techniques, thought processes, and other essentials of leadership, the only way someone actually becomes a great and meaningful leader is if he is willing to, and capable of, motivating others to follow his lead. Maya Angelou said, "Be a rainbow to someone else's cloud," and while that is wonderful advice for all of us, it is essential for anyone that wishes to truly lead. Leaders must at all times exhibit a steady, comforting, and continuous positive attitude and can- do approach.

1. How do true leaders inspire? Many seem to think that inspiration comes as a result of their rhetoric, as if beautiful words, and lofty expressions, are what motivates others. In fact, true leaders need not be great orators (although it is certainly, at times, beneficial), but rather must inspire others by what they do, and what they represent. False leaders often underestimate the acumen of their constituents, and fail to realize that unless one's actions are consistent with their lovely words, people recognize this inconsistency. The greatest leaders are invariably the one's that inspire others by being the type of person that they are. Traits that inspire include: absolute integrity; extraordinary effort; positive attitude and manner; showing genuine gratitude; assuming personal responsibility (never blame); and effective listening. While these are merely some of the traits, they are the most easily observed by even casual observers, and therefore are necessities for inspirational leadership. Leaders who inspire find others more willing to follow them.

2. How can a leader motivate? One of the easiest ways is, of course, leading by example. Human nature is such that people are far more willing to, and apt to, listen to, and thus follow, someone that walks the walk, instead of merely talking the talk. Another way to motivate is to always thank

people for whatever they are willing and able to do, to assist the leader and the organization. Reality is that almost every organization sees some version of the 80/ 20 rule, which means that at least eighty percent of the work and effort is done by less than twenty percent of the members. Therefore, great leaders must truly appreciate what these people do. They must also be grateful for those that simply belong, because they are also helping by providing both numbers (strength in numbers), plus generally a certain degree of needed revenue.

Leaders can only motivate and inspire when they commit to providing value, and commit to their best efforts, and absolute integrity. This is, of course, another reason that there are so few truly great leaders.

LEADERSHIP IS MORE OF A PRACTICE THAN THEORY

Leadership is more about practice than theory, even if theory can inform some relevant insights as part of a leadership development programme.

Great leaders lead by example, not just talk or orders. Leading by example will garner respect and admiration from the troops as well as compliance. In a network marketing company, recruits join voluntarily so it's up to them whether they will follow you or quit. You can't use force or order them around like a boss does in a traditional job.

The best way to get recruits to do things is to motivate them with their goals dangling in front of them like a carrot by remind them why they joined. Praise a good recruit generously in front of others, with hold praise to others who don't perform or try. Reward good recruits with plagues, certificates, trophies, awards etc. in front of the entire team. Keep everyone on the same page by making sure everyone knows what the company's purpose is and why they should work hard to reach their individual goals.

It's not easy being a leader, and there is a lot to live up to. When you are in a leadership position people are watching you, they watch your every move, and since humans like to imitate, and since you are in a position of authority and power, something that they might themselves aspire to, they copy your every move.

Now then, what if you were told that; "if you aren't leading by example, then you are indeed unfit to lead," and in that case you shouldn't be in the leadership authoritative position in the first place. Is that too over the top, does that offend you, or are you one with that persona? The reason for this question is simple; there are far too many people living in hypocrisy, busy running around telling other people what to do. That isn't leadership, that's a disaster waiting to happen. If you run a company, sports team, or are involved in education, politics, nonprofit groups, or any other human endeavor involving leadership you need to understand why leading by example is the proper motif.

Okay so, how does one lead by example? Well, a lot of it has to do with integrity. If you want your team to look spiffy, then you must dress the part. If you want your team to get along, you must be a personable individual. If you demand excellence, you must strive for excellence in everything you do yourself. If you want to uphold the company image, you can't show up to work in a dirty car. You may think that's going too far, but rest assured it's not. In fact, all eyes are upon you if you are the leader, and if you care about doing it correctly you must set the example. If you don't, you're doing a disservice to your team, and you are living in hypocrisy.

THE UNDERSTANDING OF THE EMOTIONS OF OTHERS AND HOW TO REACT TO THEM

The leader acts as the emotional guide for his or her followers. The effect of the leader on the followers is often astounding. For example, an effective leader normally possesses high levels of persuasion. However, it is not the level of persuasion that is always evident. You will see when people's emotions are infused with enthusiasm, their performance will soar. On the other hand, if they are exposed to anxiety and resentment, they will not perform as well.

The mechanisms behind this phenomenon are worthy of understanding. Much of this has got to do with the design of the human brain. Our emotional centers operate in an open loop system. This means that it depends on external sources to manage itself. This enables us to come to the emotional rescue of other people. It is the mechanism that enables us to be empathetic. A good example is a mother soothing an upset child.

Research in intensive care units has revealed that the comforting presence of a loved one will help to lower the blood pressure of the patient. This open loop design of our limbic system means that other people can change our emotions. Understanding this in leadership is vital.

For example, if the leader is frustrated, this will be picked up by the followers in spite of the leader's attempt to disguise it, even if nothing is said. Open communication is the only antidote to this problem. It requires frank discussions between the leader and the staff, laced with a bit of humor, to establish understanding so that the negative contagious effect does not take place.

Studies have shown how emotions are contagious and spread whenever people are near each other. This takes place even if the contact is completely non-verbal. The more cohesive the group, the more it is possible to "catch" emotional feelings from others in the group.

In the workplace, the leader plays a pivotal role in setting the emotional standards for the group day by day.

Not all emotions spread at the same rate or with the same effect. At one end of the scale cheerfulness, warmth and humor are very contagious. On the other hand, grumpiness, depression and gloom do not spread at the same rate. Laughter is very contagious because when we hear laughter we automatically smile which spreads a chain reaction throughout the group.

Laughter is very potent because it instantly creates a lock between limbic systems. This means that it is the most direct communication possible between two people. Laughter sends a powerful message that we are on the same wavelength. We trust and comfort each other.

This is like saying that if the leader is unhappy, so is the team. This has been demonstrated many times with coaches and sports teams.

Knowing the value of humor, laughter and influence should we totally reconsider the way we teach, train and develop our leaders? Should we be training them in this skill of unspoken influence that is so powerful? Should we be selecting people for leadership positions who have a sense of humor and a sense of fun?

As a Leader, some component of your emotional intelligence is represented by social intelligence which implies understanding the way the others feel and somehow control and manage the emotions and behavior of the respective persons. Once you get to "polish" your social intelligence you will be able to better interact with those around you.

Below there is a list of the benefits one can enjoy when being endowed with social intelligence:

• maintaining good relationships;

• making a good impression on others;

• asking a favor from a person without creating an uncomfortable feeling;

• calming a person down;

• helping others in need;

• selling an idea or a product;

• Making a large network of friends and easily interact with new people, making the groups better connect among them.

• Navigate the shift towards team-oriented work relationships

Team relations is one indispensable part in organization's development, which managers could strongly emphasize in their plans. However, they themselves must have recognized and trained in much of an ever changing teamwork dynamic.

Having done so, they would then nurture them in an organization, and later turn their scrutinizing eyes on future staff -during interviews and, as key emphasis in staff workshops. Some of the key workshop ingredients could be learning sessions in conflict resolution, negotiation and stress management.

Otherwise, without health team relations, staff performance can be adversely affected as there might be reduced morale to work in a conflictual work environment, high toll on the mental health dysfunctioning of workers; confusion, disengagement, absenteeism and dismissals of affected staff by their unsuspecting bosses.

In teams, however, conflicts are the most infectious yet inevitable challenges. There can always be strategy-based and content-based disagreements. Regular meetings have been known to be best remedy for organizations and groups marred with conflicts. It can also mean bringing to the table every arising individual-concern for solution-finding to avoid spill-over effect.

Modalities thought to best work for specific interventions must be discussed before executing the tasks in line with them. There are teams that could be "shrewd" enough to come out with suitable structures, forming suitable operations guidelines and systematic steps -with which to successfully implement organization programs, even when their initiatives contradict the organization ones - conceivable "not to be smart" enough; so long as in the end, anticipated organization goals are met. For order ya jjesi, it could be different matter, just as in organizations with overly centralized management systems.

While in the meeting, it is best when each member makes a contribution or suggestion; the most quiet members ought to speak or be encouraged too. For justice assurance, also, equal time for everyone to express strongly held views should be allocated.

At the beginning of meetings agendas can be created basing on key contentious areas in team relations; the causes of arguments, have discussions done around them, followed by agreements and ways forward.

While expecting that at the end of the meeting, conflicting team members re-think their positions and realign themselves with the rest of the team's mainstream one. However, care must be taken to ensure equal platform for everyone to air out his or her views.

In a team, it is all about consulting each other before action, reporting the action to the rest of the members, and involving them in any plan -whose outcome could affect them all. Every member must have either participated in the plans or sought to be furnished with information about it.

Some organizations may have a culture or history of nurturing all staff equally to become leaders -starting from the team situation. However, one wonders how everyone can be leader within a team of five people. What a test! It is usually difficult one, unless all members are given clear roles structures for them to play and achieve through.

In spite of that, there is always a tendency of one member in the team emerging dominant, and later imposing himself or herself on the team as overall decision-maker. Nature must have provided that; for anything to function normally, there must be a leader no matter how that leader comes to exist as one. It is such mysterious circumstances that even make people (spiritualists) think leadership is from God.

It is possible to realize group cohesion, enthusiasm, high commitment, high involvement, high performance, lessened achievement resistance, and easy conflict resolution if the organization presented alternative options (of members) for every team to elect its own leader.

However, set guidelines must be given to the electoral or appointing authority to ensure that a leader chosen suits the organization culture and history, and has its current vision and expected strength to grasp and execute tasks. But the approach could change with well oriented team members; aware of their roles in fulfilling objectives of daily field goals throughout the program time.

Where a team leader option is additionally considered by the organization, he or she should be charismatic enough to generate morale, solidarity and enthusiasm in the team-situation amidst field challenges.

In that regard, presence of a team-leader should not mean passivity for him or other team members, but active role play even when the rest of the team are burnt-out. There can be a tendency of over-functioning members of the team unconsciously lessening work-involvement of other team members. It is therefore a team-leaders' continued efforts that will, time and again, resuscitate the fatigued members' work-spirits; to push on, until the end of the field program.

Each member, as having equal life challenges that may be economic or career-related, must put in equal effort in relation to his or her distinct role. And, of course, the concrete tasks and responsibilities must be those that help the team, exactly, to achieve its set goals -reviewable at all meeting held regularly for enthusiasm raising.

Like in any other purposeful relationships, there must be specific values nurtured to bond members in light with the work they do. These could be; mutual respect, mutual responsibility, cooperation, listening and sharing -a kind of sisterly or brotherly relationship.

Where work conditions are not acceptable, and team pressure is channeled onto one person, very soon, it would cause agony -a feeling of injustice and a constant struggle to realize a comfortable position in the team and states within oneself. But, still, the element of competition can always erupt.

Different individuals will want to gather pomp, and searching for all they are best in and testing them on others' ability. This is when the tendency to disrespect, error-searching, and to making endless criticisms ensue, but with strong and focused leadership of one entrusted for the task - be it at team and organization level, all such could be contained. This can help save affected members from feelings of intellectual injustice, work-place insecurities, low work involvement, and negative field outcomes and reports,.

If team's dysfunctionality arises from the organizational structure and turns out to victimize team-members, then cooperation with a leader -who receives and listens to member complaints, keeps confidential information, ensures field-work constraints are included in the final report -along with specific recommendations that addresses them in future, becomes ideal.

In circumstances where the team is multi-racial, certain individual members' actions can be interpreted as offensive so much that those offended opt to grieve silently - wondering if the "offender" really meant it or not. Such confusion created amidst work tasks -supposed to be done, can be very agonizing while at the same time too, results into negative end-of-term report.

When ill-feelings are brought to the team leader's attention, he or she expectedly convenes meetings aimed at seeking explanations and clarity of the troublesome statements made or actions done, while ensuring that the offended members understand the cultural gaps or differences.

And such explanations related to culture ought to be made clear; both prior field placement and in daily group reviews of work done. To note is that learning process highly varies sharply; from on that is instant, one-day realization to weeks, months acknowledgment to years. Beyond that; it turns out to be an abnormality.

There, also, can be a time when work pressure is so overwhelming that members lose grip on work, tempers rise easily, and burn-out sets in. While in this situation the focus need to be; compromise, in the best interest of meeting project goals within the set period of time. But, as opportunities arise for friendly or casual discussions, dissatisfaction can be aired out politely, and with respect.

Alternatively, one could buy time until the end of the project so that as the bosses applaud them for the excellent field-work at the end of the year, the team ensures availability of time to air out the other side of the coin missing in the general report summary, though already stated in the detailed one.

It is helpful too to help colleagues adjust, learn or improve, no matter how arrogant they might be. This, as already pointed out, can occur immediately or even very long after the end of the program. Then, perhaps, the kind helper could receive a telephone call, card or nice gifts in appreciation. Of course, anyone would like to be honored.

It is a time when those oppressed in the team will want to get some airtime or breather to speak about what did not go well in the field. They could have chose compromise or to lose at hot arguments in the field, and win later (out of the field).

Calling for individual member reports alongside the main one presented by the team leader, too, could be excellent.

This ensures that anomalies are never left to rot -to no reinstatement, but addressed as they arise.

Unfortunately or fortunately, every person nurses specific biases, social stereotypes and certain obsessions. With time, such attitudes lead to caucuses within the team, in which members find comfort -as they move to the field station, and during work breaks.

With time, some can be really nagging, especially when the obsessions -be it in ideology, culture and other behavioral specifics are perennial, where somebody continues saying the same statement every time at the pace of two minutes as though he or she has lost her mind. Anyway, reports say there moments when people are not at their best, and how quick they return to normal is what makes anyone unique.

Others may be sort of intellectual imperialists, who want to selfishly impose their views on a group at all cost and have them work in the team as general rules. Interestingly, they could even "steal" other members' ideas and make them their own -to give the imperialist's impression of a powerful figure that is manifested all the time. Indeed, it is debilitating working with the same person throughout the years yet, already, every day to the victimized person can be like a year!

But also the group leader could ensure that times are set for group parties, casual-conversational meetings and talking about a wide areas of life, this time round, outside work arena -while constantly encouraging members to open up to such occasions.

The team leader must endure the trouble of appealing to members to share knowledge, rather than compete about who has best strategist. But because the focus, then, is about registering team results, such happy moments could be only ended by reviewing project objectives and setting next days' timeline.

In addition, the team leader could encourage sincere guidance rather than mere criticism, ridicule or sizing up of others in the team, and the same be the case with the parent organization's top management; ensuring that members report ill-feelings as well as physical illnesses that could be misinterpreted by the group as pretense or laziness.

While those with cherished ideas they wish other team members could adopt, gently and patiently explain how good they are since, as noted earlier, it sometimes takes longer time for people to understand, appreciate and adopt something new. And, as part of the team work ethic, mutual consultation ought to be encouraged -to avoid unnecessary criticisms and endless complaints -due to blunders and errors during role execution.

There has never been a leader who knew everything that he would ever need to know, had all the experiences, expertise, judgment and wisdom, or was able to do it all alone, without the assistance of others. Great leaders must not only motivate others to follow and participate, but he must also engage those with needed skills, expertise, experiences, judgment and/ or wisdom that might be able to potentially enhance his ability to be a truly effective leader. Colin Powell stated, "Endeavors succeed or fail because of the people involved. Only by attracting the best people will you accomplish great goals." I have discovered, however, that far too many involved in leadership appear to feel threatened in some way, by those that might have more expertise than they have. However, our most effective leaders understand that great leadership is not about ego or personal gratification, but rather about doing the best and most effective job in terms of assisting an organization reach its maximum potential.

1. It is essential that a leader create a reliable and knowledgeable inner circle of trusted advisers that he can trust, rely upon, and turn to when he has questions, doubts, needs some sort of clarification, or simply needs a sounding board. Unfortunately, far too many in leadership surround themselves solely with others who either agree with them, or will simply be diplomatic yes - men. While it may make someone feel superficially better to hear others agree, that is not what a true leader needs. Only when his advisers challenge him, question him, even perhaps play the Devil's advocate at times, can a leader thoroughly examine a situation, his options, and better understand the ramifications of actions.

2. It is important for a leader to understand that no one, even the wisest and most experienced individual, ever has all the questions. It is not only perfect alright for a leader to ask others their opinions and turn for advice, but doing so invariably creates better and stronger leadership. The quality of these advisers, the diversity of their backgrounds, points of view, ways they look at things, etc., immensely impact how well a leader will perform.

True leadership must never be about an individual's ego, frailties, or insecurities. A real leader always puts doing the right thing highest, and sets goals based on a vision that he holds essential and important. Perhaps this is one explanation of why it is often so difficult to find actual leaders.

Leadership is a big word. It means more than what it appears to be and is written about in millions of books around the world. Leading a person or a group of people is an infinite responsibility. Of course, we have different kinds of leaders and people are constantly looking for leaders who can create more leaders than followers. At work, in business, in families and within friends, leaders are important because they just don't show directions but help people identify their strengths and bring out the best in them.

Supreme quality work is one of the main attributes of management or leadership.

Quality management is crucial for the people involved as it is for the end result of any work. Managing the quality of the team does not always have to do with work. It also means maintaining a healthy, cheerful, enthusiastic and result-oriented atmosphere within a team. Great managers always focus on creating a code of honor for the team before they get started. It is an excellent, result-oriented and an effective way to lay rules that everybody in the team must play by. It is unspoken on many occasions but firmly agreed by all. It is largely true that when there are no rules, people come up with their own. This is perhaps the most deterring factor between good and great quality management.

Quality management is a vital aspect for any team improvement.

Quality management deals with empowering people and encouraging open communication at all times. Of course, the code of honor presets how issues and concerns within the team must be addressed constructively. As for work, clear and sharp communication helps members of the team comprehend the true reason for their presence and how their work affects others' and the team as a whole. No two people are alike in a team and therefore the approach to handle each of them and their work must be different too. Where there are people, there is bound to be friction however here are some basic recommendations for improving quality management within a team.

Consistent Improvement:

Time is more important and valuable than money. This cannot be stressed enough. In the world of finance, a golden rule explains that a dollar today is more valuable than a dollar tomorrow. Similarly, in the team management, the quality of the team's work along with interpersonal relationships must improve on a consistent basis. Everybody appreciates an overnight success but unless it is a consistent story, nobody wants to own it. The dynamics of people, the quality of the commitment towards work and team work must improve at regular intervals. Continuous improvement shows the capacity of the team to withstand pressure.

Customer of the mind: If it was not for the customer, there would be no business. Without business or work, any of this would not make sense. Quality is a feeling more than it is a tag. Teams need to be made understood that when any customer receives a product or service or even interact with the staff, he or she must feel the quality. Quality is present in all that can be done and all that cannot be done. As long as team members can put themselves in customers' shoes and feel the difference, positive changes are limited. A simple greeting can stand out for quality and get the conversation going. When teams have customers on their mind, accountability and sense of pride helps them deliver only the best.

Get Involved:

A feedback mechanism is one of the best ways to take appropriate actions. When quality work is the focus, it is always beneficial to get all members of the team involved. Typically, the people who interact with the customers are the best to give the feedback about what the customer wants. Customers are always giving feedback with their emails, gestures, attitudes and voices. Only the best trained quality obsessed teams can identify and act on that feedback. Involving everyone will broaden the possibility of getting more solutions and ways to improve quality within a team.

Recognition:

When a member of a team goes out of his/her way to help resolve a customer issue, be present in place of another team member or stand for the mission of the team, recognition is a great way to show appreciation. Just like businesses appreciates great financial results and reviews by top notch companies, team members also appreciate being recognized for their efforts. Lack of recognition can lead to discouragement and affect the morale of any great bonded team.

Quality management is largely based upon how the leader views it, the team members view it and how the management views it. As long as these three entities are in sync with their definition and belief about quality, the business will continue to thrive under the most severe of circumstances.

HOW TO MANAGE CONFLICTS

To be frank, disagreement and conflict are normal in the work place and among people. Although leaders don't like conflict, they are however advised to face it with positive attitude.

When disagreement occurs, being the leader, you need to take proactive action. Never sit and wait there. You need to take fast action to identify the cause for conflict so that you can find constructive solution within the shortest period of time. If you don't have much experience in leading people through conflicts, here are some useful tips for you.

Avoiding issues doesn't make them go away; they continue to exist and grow whether one pays attention to them or not.

In today's politically correct environment, we seem to be encouraged to get along under all circumstances. That is unrealistic, especially in a business setting in which revenue streams are vital and competition is high. Moreover, it is unrealistic to expect human beings to always agree and equally unrealistic to expect new ideas and change to go unchallenged. Conflict is bound to exist in every level of an organization. In fact, it is necessary for growth, natural to human behavior, and normal. However, there are two important points to keep in mind. First, conflict is part of change and growth and need not be avoided. Second, and even more important, leaders and potential leaders need to know how to manage conflict productively. Conflicts can lead to intense emotional responses between people and organizations. Protracted and unaddressed conflict within an organization leads to damaged work relationships; a culture of distrust; and an environment plagued by disgruntled employees, high turnover, and missed opportunities.

The key to managing conflict constructively is to identify and address issues early, before they reach a level of intractability. Conflict management competent means you recognize the importance of managing and resolving conflict constructively. Conflict management competent leaders support a business culture of conflict-competence and practice it throughout their teams and organizations.

- Consider the timing

Most of the people tend to be emotional when issues arise. When the emotions run high, it is not the right time to discuss any matter. You had better consider taking a break from the discussion, say 30 minutes or an hour. For serious issues which involve many parties, it would be good if you can put the matter aside for a day or two. Let everyone to calm down. You need to keep in mind that upset people do not solve problem well. Anger causes anger. Hence, there is no point for us to keep arguing or quarreling. Being a superior, it is important for you to break the emotional cycle immediately so that the working relationship between you and your subordinates will not be spoilt.

- Show that you are open-minded

Subordinates do not want to share their views if they know that their superiors are close-minded and stubborn. On the other hand, they are more willing to voice their opinions if they know that their leaders are willing to listen to them. You are advised to listen to your subordinates' point of view from time to time. Let them know that you are open-minded. Let them know you appreciate their contribution. You need to treat every subordinate fairly. Please keep in mind that every staff has the same right to provide comments and feedback.

- Use your authority as the last resort

People disagree with themselves for different reason depending on the level of life or organization they find themselves. As a leader, you are the last person to which everything comes and whatever decision you make will make the difference, so it is essential that you understand the reason for the conflict and find the best possible solution to keep all parties happy with your decision. Sometimes your decision wouldn't be in favor of any party, yes, that's why you are the leader. You shouldn't be judgmental and bias with your final decision.

LEADERSHIP STARTS FROM WITHIN

With countless books on developing leadership skills, a myriad of articles each with the best strategy on how to effectively lead, and hundreds of social media sites that strive to improve one's leadership abilities, one stops and wonders: Where do I start? How do I choose the best strategies and approaches with people whom I manage and lead? And how do I know that these strategies and approaches are the best?

The best way is start developing your leadership capabilities is from within yourself. With all the before mentioned leadership tools, it's very easy to lose the focus, and invest your energies in learning new leadership skills and models rather than investing your energies in building you. Ken Blanchard and Mark Miller (2004) compares leadership to an iceberg - 20% of leadership is what we see - skills or "doing", and 80% is what we cannot see - leader's character or "being". Thus, "starting from within" and developing one's character is a fundamental basis of effective leadership.

Great leaders know themselves very well. Know your strengths and your challenges, and embrace your challenges. Once one embraces and acknowledges them, one's challenges become a cornerstone for professional and personal development. It's almost paradoxical; the more ownership we take over our challenges, the less a challenge and more a strength they become. The process of working through our challenges takes humility, and many times it means asking for help from others who have gone through a similar process. Thus, always ask for help from someone whose leadership skills you respect.

Always know where you are going and where you would like to get to. One cannot lead people not knowing their own direction. In simple terms, stick to the mission and assess the "big picture". Whether you are leading 600 people or 2 people, it is important to step away mentally (and sometimes physically) from daily operations, place daily problems in a perspective, assess and focus on the ultimate goal of you and your followers.

Be truthful about your motivation and intentions. Ask yourself "Why am I leading, and do I believe in the course and the mission of my organization?" The people whom you are leading will be loyal to the organization and believe in the mission only to the degree that you do. "Everything rises and falls on leadership" (Blanchard & Miller, 2004).

Never lead out of fear. In dealing with daily challenges, it is sometimes easy to lose the focus, and base our decisions on our fears: a possible loss of a contract, client, or an employee. It's important to take into consideration all factors and possible consequences while making leadership and business decisions; however the best decisions are those that serve the ultimate organizational goals rather than serving single interests or situations.

Leadership is never a task, and always a process. Thus, while you are embracing this wonderful and very challenging process, always keep You in focus.

HOW TO GAIN DEEP INSIGHT INTO LEADERSHIP'S CRITICAL ROLE IN ORGANIZATION HEALTH

The rapid growth of the economic environment as well as the emergence of the internet made it easier to communicate with countries around the world. This in turn changed the business environment in every country, causing a competitiveness in the market that increases with each passing year (Friedman, 2007). In order to keep their business afloat, business owners discovered they had to offer better quality products at a lower cost, employ strategies that were uniquely suited for the organization to adapt according to current business trends and also flexibility in facing the rapid change of the business environment. Effective leadership is one of most essential parts of the overall method for an organization to sustain their business in the face of problems caused by the rapid growth of the economic environment. (CabezaErikson, Edwards, and Van Brabant, 2008) Leaders are the one who control and take charge of the operation of an organization and good leaders are able to set optimistic goals and objectives while steering the operation of the company towards those goals through effective strategies. Other than that, good leaders can also influence their employees and motivate them by strengthening a positive organization culture and through generous employee benefits, for instance health care insurance, worker compensation, leave benefit and others.

Intelligent leaders also have the responsibility to use their skills and knowledge to effectively and efficiently guide their business forward in the face of an uncertain future and also to decrease the feelings of insecurity in their employees caused by that uncertainty. A leader has the power to influence the success of the organization, due to his full power to control the direction of the organization, as well as through the influence they exert on their employees that motivates them to bring the company to greater heights.

Effective leadership

Leadership is a kind of power where one person has the ability to influence or change the values, beliefs, behaviour and attitudes of another person (Ganta, and Manukonda, 2014). A person with strong leadership ability will be a good example or role model to their employees, because the leader who is able to effectively achieve some good result or achievement gains the trust and admiration of their employees, and inadvertently changes their values, beliefs, behaviour and attitudes, for mimicry is the sincerest form of flattery (Grint, 2007). This statement is also supported by Northhouse (2009), who states that leaders who possess strong leadership have the strength to influence others to achieve the goals and objectives of the organization. Other than that, there is also another way to define a leader that has strong leadership. A characteristic of effective leaders is that they give a clear direction to their employees, and also lead their employees to commit to their jobs and to work as a group to achieve the organization's goals and objectives (Wasim, and Imran, 2010). This also tells us that good leaders usually have a clear vision for the company and therefore can easily identify the problems and obstacles that currently stand between them and the aims of the organization. In this way they are able to effectively and efficiently bring about the necessary reforms that will bring the company into the future while keeping abreast with contemporary changes in the business world. According to Jackson and Parry (2008), leadership is a process where leaders use their skills and knowledge to lead and bring a group of employees in the desired direction that is relevant to their organization's goals and objectives. Additionally, an effective leader that has strong leadership skills should also be in possession of certain characteristic, such as, passion, consistency, trust and vision; for only leaders who own these characteristics are able to build trust in employees.

Leadership and management are two different aspects, management is more like the traditional way of managing business, which the owner of the business has complete control of the organization, and will singlehandedly establish a direction and direct their employees to do their work in accordance to the owner's instruction and plan. On the other hand, leadership is when the leader guides their employees towards the organizational goals, all the while trying to communicate and motivate their employees in order to make sure their employees are in the right position to use their talents and commit to their jobs. Leadership strategies also will change according to the current trends when necessary, unlike management that merely follows it's old, traditional rules. (Graetz et al., 2010)

Change management

Change has always been an issue for organization, just as it has always been a common characteristic of human life. Change is definitely hard for humans to accept as it is something that pull people out of their comfort zones, which forces them to change their habits and makes them highly uncomfortable (Lorenzoni, Nicholson, and Whitmarsh, 2007). For example, a worker usually starts work at 9 a.m.; if his supervisor suddenly requests the worker to begin work at 7 a.m., the worker will be late to work because force of habit keeps him waking up late. The same thing applies to the organization, if an employee's normally does their work following the sequence of A to Z, suddenly changing the sequence of work from Z to A, can be quite difficult for all the employees to get use to in a short period of time.

Change management in an organization can be defined as an approach to deal with change in two different areas - the organization and the individual, with individuals and the overall organization adapting to change at their own pace and style (Rouse, 2014). Change management allows the organization to catch an opportunity to gain a competitive advantage, if the organization effectively and efficiently implements and adapts to the change of the market (Du Plessis, 2007). There are three stages in change management, which are adapting to change, controlling the change and lastly effecting the change. The first stage, adapting to change, is determining the individual readiness to adapt to the changes and their willingness to commit to the change. The second stage involves controlling the change and implementing it in daily life. Lastly, effecting the change, is to sustain the change and to get used to it in life. (Hritz, 2008)

The time taken for the process of change management in an organization is hard to determine, due to the difference in individual employees' ability to adapt, as some might rapidly embrace change, while others might take a longer time to engage in the change. Just like some employees will be happy with the change, and some might not. The leader should communicate and work together with the group of employees to sustain the long term process changes (Wuestman and Casey, 2015).

Change factor lead by leadership

In terms of leadership, it is defined as the ability to influence a group of employees' values, beliefs, attitudes and behavior. (Ganta, and Manukonda, 2014). A leader with strong leadership skills can easily motivate and influence the employees of the organization and apply effective changes to the organization. According to Atkinson, if there is no effective leadership in an organization no changes will be made, because there are no leaders that motivate and lead the organization's employees as well as provide a clear direction for the organization (Atkinson, 2015).

a) Trust - Trust is an essential issue in leadership for leaders, as gaining the trust of group members or employees could help to improve the overall performance and commitment of the group members or employees (Lee et al., 2010). If the employees or the group members trust in their leaders, it reflects that they are good, effective leaders. Only when the employees trust in their leader will change be brought about, because people will only follow a person that they trust to lead them to the correct path; not a leader that only talks but without action to back up their words (Stacey , Paul and Alice, 2011). If the employees trust their leader, this relationship will bind them together and improve the overall performance and commitment of the employees; if it happens conversely, the performance and commitment of the employees will go downhill and could cause a high employee turnover rate in the organization.

b) Organizational Culture - Leadership can shape a good culture. A culture is shaped within the trust between the employees and the leaders of an organization, or it can defined as cultures need trust to be able to form. Employees and leaders in the organization need to trust each other in order to shape a positive organizational culture. Leaders with strong leadership skills are able to shape a positive culture in the organization (Ionescu, 2014), due to them being able to inspire trust from their employees. A positive organizational culture not only improves 2Global Journal of Management and Business Research Volume XV Issue IX Version I Year ( ) A 2015 © 2015 Global Journal 1 s Inc. (US) How Effective Leadership can Facilitate Change in Organizations through Improvement and Innovation performance, but also influences the behavior and attitude of the employees in the organization for the better. In addition, it motivates employees and gives them a sense of belonging to the organization, which inspires loyalty and commitment to the company (Schein, 2010). A good organizational culture not only improves the performance and reduces the turnover rate of the organization, it also facilitates the solution of internal issues in the organization. When a good organizational culture is established, that does not discriminate based on races, religious and etc, it provides a pleasant environment to work in, thereby reducing internal conflict and encouraging discussion and cooperation in order to work through any interemployee issues that crop up. In addition, good organizational culture encourages a sense of healthy competition, motivating employees in the organization to be more innovative. Therefore, a strong organizational culture can change the overall performance of the organization.

c) Learning - An effective leader can encourage employees in the organization to learn through certain types of motivators, such as rewards or position (Azzam, 2014). Continuously learning is one of the ways to improve the overall performance of the organization. It is not only the employees that need to improve but even all segments of the leadership levels of an organization, if only to set a good example to the bottom line to motivate them to learn. Leaders should join leadership training programs in order to strengthen their skills and knowledge, making them more effective in their strategies and execution (Freifeld, 2013). The same goes for employees, as sending employees for further training will improve their ability to do their job as well as help to facilitate the effective implementation of the desired changes. This helps the organization to increase the productivity and performance of the employees (Abou-Moghli, 2015). Since learning does not have an end, leaders need continuous improvement of their leadership skills and knowledge to be competitive in the business market nowadays (Park, et al., 2014). If an organization or leader stops improving and as a result find that their skills and knowledge are insufficient, their company will surely find itself deteriorating. The organization, Nokia, is a very good example, Nokia was once one of the best cell phone brands in the world, but Nokia did not continuously improve their skills and make changes in order to adapt to the new trends and needs of the market, and Nokia dropped from the one of the best to a brand that not many people pay attention to (Lee, 2013).

d) Teamwork, Communication and Leading - Besides strengthening their leadership skills, leaders also need to encourage the employees of the organization to be innovative and cooperative. Teamwork and communication are the best way to create innovative ideas in order to produce the best outcome for the organization (Maxwell, 2009). To achieve the kind of teamwork and rapport that is necessary for the birth of innovative ideas, leaders need to cultivate a positive culture where the employees trust each other , are allowed to do their own jobs without too much interference and have the freedom to establish a dialogue with one another (Malloch and Melnyk, 2013). Leaders that wish to facilitate effective change in the organization should encourage employees to collaborate and communicate with each other, for this is how people are able to create and discover new ways to think (Gilley, Dixon and Gilley, 2008), which produces a greater outcome for the organization and also encourages them to learn from different people the ways to improve themselves. Even high ranking management can learn from the strong points of their employees, which they might find themselves lacking. Communication helps people to get to know each other, and also could help to create more new ideas by sharing opinions with each other. It is also one of the best ways to gain each other's trust and bond the whole employees in the organization together. Lastly, leadership not only influence the employees in the organization, but also provides a clear direction to the employees according to the organization's vision and mission. Effective leaders set strategies to help the employees to achieve the company's target and objectives. Leader also play a role in monitoring the direction of the employees to make sure the employees are on the right path to achieve the goals according to the strategies. This is only possible with effective leadership that inspires employee trust, as employees are unwilling to follow someone who has little to no idea of what they are doing and who wastes too much time and resources on the unnecessary.

Discussion

Effective leadership plays an important role in managing a business in the current business environment, for the old ways of business management are not enough to sustain a company in the modern market. Although leadership and management are two completely different systems, an organization might be surprised to find that there is no one system that completely suits their needs, so it advisable that they focus on the skills that are suitable for their organization. Management is a system that is based more on planning, budgeting and controlling. The organization is emphasizes on following the plan that is set by the upper rank executives in the organization, and following their orders to solve problems. Leadership focuses more on guiding the employees, leading them in the desired direction, according to the organization vision and © 2015 Global Journals Inc. (US) 3Global Journal of Management and Business Research Volume XV Issue IX Version I Year 2015 ( ) A How Effective Leadership can Facilitate Change in Organizations through Improvement and Innovation mission while communicating with and motivating them to complete their tasks. Under leadership, the boss guides and works together with their employees to produce their desired outcome; while old style management orders employees to follow directives while the upper management is focused on planning and both are separate and do not work together. Besides that, the current business environment requires organization to make changes in order to keep up with the rapid changes in the business environment. If the organization fails to make changes in order to adapt to the market they will fail to survive and will face bankruptcy. Leadership is in charge of providing a clear vision and a systematic way to effective achieve that vision, for if there is no leadership there is no change in organization management (Atkinson, 2015). Although leadership can bring lots of changes and increase the organization's performance, but in reality there are more factors to consider that might affect the possibility of the changes to occur. Every employees' behavior and attitudes are different, some employees might be able to easily adapt to the change but some will resist the change; some might accept the ways of their leaders and learn from the action of their leaders but some will become jealous of their leaders and refuse to cooperate. This would drag the performance of the organization down. Effective leadership is the best way to managing changes though it must be remembered that there are no problem solving solutions that are perfect and that issues will still be faced that cannot be fixed.

MOTIVATE AND INSPIRE TO BREAK THROUGH THE PERVASIVE NEW CYNICISM

Cynicism in government is equally prevalent. Lawless (2015) states that "the overwhelming majority of 13-25 year olds view the political system as ineffective, broken, and downright nasty. As a consequence, nine out of 10 will not even consider running for office."

So, how do leaders infuse others with "life and energy and passion" when cynicism abounds?

How can they inspire people to join them in noble or even fanciful ventures when those potential followers reject idealism and enthusiasm, mistrust authority, or simply do not believe change can occur?

We can begin by looking at cynicism itself

Steven Colbert said: "Cynicism masquerades as wisdom, but it is the farthest thing from it. Because cynics don't learn anything. Because cynicism is a self-imposed blindness, a rejection of the world because we are afraid it will hurt us or disappoint us."

Cynicism may be a culprit, but it serves many purposes. It frees us from unrealistic expectations. It shields us from the hurt and disappointment of idealism. It allows us to make light of people or circumstances that can bring harm.

In an amusing but thought-provoking article called Positive Cynicism, Richard Bayan acknowledges that cynicism bestows some benefits on the practitioner, but he suggests that it can lead to "alienation, depression and pervasive pessimism."

Cynicism also seems to have some negative health effects. One of those is heart disease (Bayan, n.d.) Another may be dementia (Firger, 2014). Cynicism also prevents individuals from enjoying opportunities that add texture and richness to their lives.

In the Bayan article previously cited, the author suggests that cynics can save themselves from the unpleasantness associated with rampant cynicism by focusing their energies on something they love. He advises cynics to recognize and live their passions while remaining skeptical.

The challenge for leaders is to break through the walls of cynicism to gain trust, to clear new paths and present new possibilities. Leaders need to bring passion into focus and to help potential followers get in touch with what is really important to them.

They must convince cynics to reject the notion that no amount of effort can bring a better future.

So, how do leaders accomplish this task?

They begin with self:

- They get in touch with their own passions. They become so focused on their own desire to make a difference that they become willing to show vulnerability in light of that passion.

- They consider what has inspired them and they build on that inspiration.
- They are authentic. They express their values and their reasons for promoting a new and different future. They let others see what matter to them.
- They suppress ego, choosing instead to concentrate on their mission and the well-being of the group.
- They recognize their own emotions and learn to manage them in ways that promote rather than hinder their cause.
- They give the best of themselves, acting as role models for everyone else. To paraphrase Ghandhi, "They become the change they wish to see."

They work with others: and through

- They readily admit challenges and work diligently to overcome them.
- They understand, acknowledge and accept the emotions of others as they attempt to minimize fear and anger brought about by uncertainty.
- They eagerly learn from others. They listen and they are passionately curious.

- They demonstrate and generate trust, which empowers others and allows their brilliance to shine.
- They expect the best from others as they give the best of themselves.

They build a culture for change:

- They create a culture that promotes success: they show what can be; they tell stories of inspiration; they engage people's imaginations and emotions; they celebrate and build up heroes .
- They analyze and focus on shared values, learning what values are important to their group and encouraging followers to act on those values.
- They deal in hope for a better future as they clearly communicate what that better future will be.
- They make their followers part of something bigger than themselves. They use "we" and "us" instead of "I" or "me."

This list seems nearly overwhelming to a new or aspiring leader or someone who has never focused on bringing excitement alive in others.

However, leaders who leave behind their own cynicism and live in a world of passion and enthusiasm eagerly embrace the actions on this list

CHAPTER 3

LEADERSHIP IN TODAY'S FAST-MOVING DIGITAL MEDIA AGE

To lead in the era of digital transformation requires individuals to be both people-oriented and technically minded (Diamanteand London, 2002). These two skills often characterize very different profiles of people that, yet, need to come together in order to implement an effective digital transformation in their organization. The case study presented by Coutu (2000), highlights the need to establish a profitable exchange relationship between leaders of people-oriented (e.g., sales), and IT functions, in order to create a cross-functional and cross-skill contamination. Systematic knowledge dissemination from the individual to the group is highlighted as the most effective way to spread knowledge and expertise across the organization (Boe and Torgersen, 2018). Coutu (2000) addresses how this cross-skill contamination can be performed, by means of implementing reverse-mentoring programs.

Nonetheless, the author uncovers the problem of potential generational conflicts, whereby newer generations, who tend to be more knowledgeable and skilled in digital technologies, may gain informational power over others, generating concern and skepticism in older, change averse, individuals (Coutu, 2000). Studying modern military operational environments, Boe and Torgersen (2018) highlight the need to lead under volatile, uncertain and complex situations, characteristics they find similarly describe the context of modern e-businesses. According to the authors, leadership training needs to combine both technology and change, creating simulations of scenarios in which ambiguous information and improvisation create complex and uncertain conditions. One way in which exposure to technology and simulations can be combined is through training in virtual spaces (Lisk et al., 2012; Lu et al., 2014). In large community games, leaders may have to recruit, motivate, reward, and retain talented team members. They have to make quick decisions that may affect their outcomes in the long-run, for which they need to analyze the environment in order to build and keep their competitive advantage (Avolio et al., 2014). Lu et al. (2014) adopt experiential learning theory (Kolb and Kolb, 2005) to explain e-leadership skills development, referring to activities in which learning is performed in a virtual context. Their study attempts to empirically examine the transferability of virtual experiences into in-role job situations.

Results show partial association between virtual games behaviors and hierarchical position of the participants, however, conclusions concerning the transferability of certain skills or experiences gained in virtual games may be highly affected by reverse causality. Ducheneaut and Moore (2005), conduct a virtual ethnography to show that people participating in multiplayer role-playing games train behaviors related to networking, management and coordination in small groups. However, in a recent review on the use of games, based on digital tools or virtual realities, for training leadership skills, Lopes et al. (2013) highlight a general lack of theoretical grounding in the development and analysis of virtual games.

Moreover, they find extant studies rarely show these games affect leadership skill outcomes (Lopes et al., 2013). Robin et al. (2011) find that while simulations facilitate learning, they do not seem to lead to better results than traditional methods. The authors suggest simulations' main advantage lies in the possibility to enable learning in situations where it would otherwise be difficult or impossible. They thus propose the use of a combination of traditional and technology-based training to achieve the most effective learning outcomes.

LEADERS' SKILLS IN THE DIGITAL ERA

Defining what skills characterize leaders in the digital era has become a matter of interest in the literature. Studies analyze what are the relevant skills e-leaders should display in order to be effective. In line with the debate on universal and contingency theories, scholars ask to what extent the skills leaders need in order to lead e-businesses differ from the ones needed in traditional organizations (Horner-Long and Schoenberg, 2002). Most studies are based on expert surveys that engage with digital experts, managers, CEOs and Managing Directors of e-businesses (Lynn Pulley and Sessa, 2001; Horner-Long and Schoenberg, 2002; Schwarzmüller et al., 2018; Sousa and Rocha, 2018). A few studies also integrate expert surveys with interviews to IT specialists (Sousa and Rocha, 2018) and C-level managers (Horner-Long and Schoenberg, 2002).

Scholars agree that the introduction of digital tools affects the design of work, and, particularly, how people work together (Barley, 2015; Schwarzmüller et al., 2018). For example, digitalization opens up new possibilities such as virtual teams and smart working, introduces new communication tools, increases speed and information access, influences power structures, and increases efficiency and standardization. In order to steer organizations and help them reap the benefits from such digital transformations, leaders may need to develop a variety of different skills. We present below the main skills leaders need in the digital transformation era that have been highlighted in the literature.

THE IMPACT OF THE DIGITAL AGE ON LEADERSHIP

Traditional skills have not been supplanted but they now co-exist with a mix of new factors.

First of all, digital leadership can be defined by a leader's contribution to the transition toward a knowledge society and their knowledge of technology. Digital leaders have an obligation to keep up with the ongoing global revolution. They must understand technology, not merely as an enabler but also for its revolutionary force.

Leadership must be driven by an attitude of openness and a genuine hunger for knowledge. Of course, no rule dictates that leaders must be literate in coding or that they graduated from machine-learning but yes, there is an imperative to understand the impact of breakthrough technologies.

Today's leaders must have the ability to identify technological trends across different sectors, such as big data, cloud computing, automation, and robotics. However, first and foremost they must possess sufficient knowledge and the vision to use these resources most effectively.

Secondly, in a knowledge society, what we do not know is as important as what we do know. Leaders should know their limits and know how to acquire missing knowledge. A leader of the future is more like a community manager rather than an authoritarian.

These days, we are observing the decline of traditional hierarchical models of organization. Take a look at how the organization of governments has changed across Western societies in recent years. A number of governments have introduced or reinforced public consultation processes as well as opened up public data for the benefit of their citizens.

These processes, by and large, will continue to grow. As a result, the hierarchical model tends to be suppressed and replaced by horizontal structures among executives, leaders from different sectors, researchers and representatives from civic society. Hierarchy fails in the digital age because it's slow and bureaucratic, whereas the new world is constantly changing and requires immediate responses.

Information is key. In today's world, power is not gained by expanding new territories or areas of influence but by deepening and widening networks and connections. But what is the role of the individual or leader, or of qualities that distinguish one grain of sand from another?

Why leaders should turn their attention to tech for good

We have to shift our focus from the threat of new technologies to the opportunities they bring.

Of course, we cannot ignore the threat of new technologies. The debate concerning the threat of technologies, especially the internet, will never end. Policymakers have proposed different ways of regulating the web, but they always are one or two steps behind. This is because law and regulations are stable and designed to be long-lasting, whereas the digital environment is changing rapidly.

We do not claim that regulation is purely ineffective, and thus we should abandon any legal solutions for creating a more secure environment. But we do suggest that we look at technologies through different lenses. We can transform the one thing that is good and bad in breakthrough technologies - the human factor.

Having acknowledged that digital technology will play a decisive role our future, leaders cannot afford to show fear or reluctance in implementing it. Instead, they must embrace technology with a clear view of its potential. We must set sail for new, ambitious lands. We choose to go to Mars because our technology enables us to at least attempt the exploration on other planets by the 2030s. And we choose to develop other fantastic things every day – self-driving cars, more powerful batteries, the Apple Watch, drones – to name only just a few.

A balanced mix of universal characteristics and digital leadership traits has the potential to guide us through years of transformation with optimism and idealism. Technology continues to prove that it can be used for the benefit of mankind, but only if we set sail on the right course and with the right companions.

DIGITAL MEDIA AND EFFECTIVE LEADERSHIP COMMUNICATION

Global connectivity and fast exchange of information have created a much more competitive and turbulent environment for e-businesses, which must deal with rapid and discontinuous changes in demand, competition and technology (Horner- Long and Schoenberg, 2002). Scholars agree that the need for speed, flexibility, and easier access to information has facilitated the adoption of flatter and more decentralized organizational structures (Horner-Long and Schoenberg, 2002). In the digital context, knowledge and information become more visible and easier to share, allowing followers to gain more autonomy (Schwarzmüller et al., 2018) and to make their voices heard at all levels of the organization (Lynn Pulley and Sessa, 2001). As information becomes more distributed within the organization, power tends to be decentralized. Digital transformation allows real-time involvement of followers in many decision processes, increasing their participation. Therefore, leaders are expected to adopt a more inclusive style of leading (Schwarzmüller et al., 2018), asking for and taking into account followers' ideas into everyday decision making, using a two-way communication and interaction. Scholars maintain that followers' higher autonomy and participation can lead to a higher sense of responsibility for the work they are accountable for. This in turn should reduce the need for control-seeking behaviors previously exerted by leaders (Horner-Long and Schoenberg, 2002; Schwarzmüller et al., 2018). At the same time, inspiring and motivating employees have become pivotal skills for leaders to master (Horner- Long and Schoenberg, 2002), and seem to be required to an even greater extent in order to encourage the continuous involvement and active participation of followers. Indeed, the same digital tools that provide autonomy to followers, may also drive them toward greater isolation (Lynn Pulley and Sessa, 2001). According to Van Wart et al. (2017) and Roman et al. (2018), some of the most common problems generated by the digitalization of organizations are worker alienation, weak social bonding, and poor accountability. It is therefore extremely important that leaders support and help followers in dealing with the challenges of greater autonomy and increased job demands, by adopting coaching behaviors that promote their development, provide resources, and assist them in handling tasks (Schwarzmüller et al., 2018).

Similarly, the ability to create a positive organizational environment that fosters a strong sense of collaboration and unity among employees has become vital for leaders to have. Yet, e- leaders' reliance on traditional social skills, such as the abilities of active listening and understanding others' emotions and points of view, may not be enough to warrant success in creating such environments. Rather, they need to integrate these social skills with the ability to master a variety of virtual communication methods (Roman et al., 2018). According to Carte et al. (2006, p. 326), "while leadership in the more traditional face-to-face context may emerge using a variety of mechanisms, in the virtual context it likely relies largely on the communication effectiveness of the leader." Roman et al. (2018, p. 5) label this skill as e-communication, and define it as "the ability to communicate via ICTs in a manner that is clear and organized, avoids errors and miscommunication, and is not excessive or detrimental to performance." The leader needs to set the appropriate tone for the communication, while organizing it and providing clear messages. Moreover, the leader needs to master different communication tools, as their communication effectiveness depends largely on the ability to choose the right communication tool. Roman et al. (2018) provide a set of major selection criteria, which includes richness of the tool, synchronicity, speed of feedback, ease of understanding by non-experts, and reprocessing capability (ability to use the communication artifact multiple times in different venues). This ability allows to adapt the communication to the receiver preferences (as it would otherwise happen in a face-to-face interaction), so as to provide a variety of cues that enhance social bonding (Shachaf and Hara, 2007; Stephens and Rains, 2011), convey the right message to the target audience, and better manage urgency and complexity.

HIGH SPEED DECISION MAKING

One way in which the introduction of technology has changed the organizational life has been the greater need for speed. Scholars agree that e-business leaders are forced to make decisions more rapidly (Lynn Pulley and Sessa, 2001; Horner-Long and Schoenberg, 2002). This seems to suggest that decisiveness, and problem-solving abilities keep being extremely relevant for e- leaders, and may become even more prominent in the future (Horner-Long and Schoenberg, 2002). According to Lynn Pulley and Sessa (2001), never-ending urgency can create situations in which leaders needs to make decisions without having all information or without having time to think and analyze the problem properly, which may lead to falling back onto habitual responses, instead of creating novel and innovative ideas. To help navigate such situations, leaders need to be able to tolerate ambiguity, while being creative at the same time (Horner-Long and Schoenberg, 2002; Schwarzmüller et al., 2018). If it is true that the digital world forces leaders to examine problems and provide innovative answers at a faster peace, the use of information technology also allows them to make more informed decisions.

Information systems can provide enormous amounts of real- time data. For this reason, the ability to process high volumes of fast-paced incoming and outgoing data (e.g., Big data), in order to analyze it, prioritize and make sense of the relevant information for decision-making, has become and will be even more relevant in the future. Recent research points out that leaders will increasingly need to collaborate with IT managers, providing directions for data analysis and offering meaningful interpretations of results (Harris and Mehrotra, 2014; Vidgen et al., 2017).

MANAGING DISRUPTIVE CHANGE

The fast-paced technological evolution places high demands on organizations' ability to deal with continuously changing conditions and players. Lynn Pulley and Sessa (2001) highlight the constant need for organizations to adapt, foresee opportunities, and sometimes improvise, in order to maintain their competitiveness in the market. Under increasing pressure to innovate, leaders need to undertake an active role in identifying the need for change, as well as handling, and initiating change within their teams and organizations (Schwarzmüller et al., 2018). Horner-Long and Schoenberg (2002) findings confirm that e-leaders tend to show more entrepreneurial and risk-taking characteristics than leaders in traditional contexts. However, continuous change should not disrupt the focus and mission of the organization. While promoting a flexible and innovative attitude in the organization, the leader needs to clarify a common direction. Lynn Pulley and Sessa (2001) identify the ability to inspire and share a common vision about the future of the organization as one of the challenges of e-leaders, who are frequently confronted with the need for change. While acknowledging the importance of this skill, Horner-Long and Schoenberg (2002) did not find it to characterize e-leaders any more than traditional leaders.

MANAGING CONNECTIVITY

Scholars maintain that e-leaders also need to foster their networking abilities. Beyond the need to explore and create networks to lobby for resources and stakeholder support (Horner-Long and Schoenberg, 2002) developing social interactions seems to play a key role in favoring innovation. As innovation becomes a top priority, leaders need to understand how to take advantage of networking opportunities (Avolio et al., 2014). The hyper-connected environment, in which leaders operate, especially with the ubiquitous use of social media and other digital platforms, provides new networking opportunities due both to an easier access to larger groups of individuals, and the possibility to establish connections through more immediate communication. New technologies and especially the advent of social networks might have reinforced the perception that being persistently part of the network is compulsory. As reported in Horner-Long and Schoenberg (2002, p. 616) "in the new economy some leaders do nothing but network - there is no commercial need. It is simply networking for networking's sake." Although it is a general requirement to be able to create and maintain social relationships with various stakeholders, effective leaders differ specifically in the ability to recognize those relationships that lead to tangible benefits (Horner-Long and Schoenberg, 2002).

THE RENAISSANCE OF TECHNICAL SKILLS

Lastly, scholars underscore the increased value of technical competencies. This represents a shift from the latest paradigm established over the past four decades, whereby leadership primarily requires emotional and social intelligence competencies that enable the leader to understand, motivate and manage his team effectively. Notwithstanding, leaders also need to understand and manage the use of various technologies. Indeed, IT knowledge and skills have become high on demand requirements to operate in a digitalized environment (Horner- Long and Schoenberg, 2002). Furthermore, the mastery of current technologies must be balanced with the ability to stay current on the newest technological developments (Roman et al., 2018). This emphasizes the need to adopt a life-long learning approach to developing one's digital skills.